www.imholtpress.com

Copyright © 2016 Peter DaTechGuy Ingemi

ANY part of this book (but not the entire book) can be reproduced and distributed for the purpose of Catholic Evangelization under the following conditions:

1. The author Peter "DaTechGuy" Ingemi is given credit
2. The Author's web site datechguyblog.com is cited
3. It is distributed free of charge
4. The mention of the publisher Imholt Press.

A portion of all sales of the paperback version of this book goes to support WQPH 89.3 Catholic Radio in Central Massachusetts.

PRINTED IN THE USA

ISBN: 978-0-9991073-0-0

THE PERFECT PROTESTANT
(AND CATHOLIC)
PRAYER

Hail Mary

DaTechGuy
Peter Ingemi

Image: The assumption. The cathedral basilica of the
Immaculate Conception Denver Colorado.

Preface

The meat of the contents of this book has been previously published as a series of blog posts at DaTechGuyBlog (http:/datechguyblog.com). I began writing it on October 6th 2015 (The feast of our Lady of the Rosary) and wrote the final piece in March of 2016. The last post went up on March 20th which, that year, was Palm Sunday.

Prior to this I had written on many topics concerning Christianity in general, and Catholicism in particular. These topics have ranged from how the shepherds of Bethlehem's appearance answered Joseph confirming **his leap of faith was correct:**

> You are Joseph, how relieved are you at this point? Remember unlike Peter he didn't have years of miracles in front of his face when he denied Christ, he only had the word of a teenage girl and a dream. There would have been little cost to him if he condemned Mary. Yet he didn't and this moment was that ultimate reward. He passed the ultimate test of faith with flying colors.

To the Fairness of Hell:

> Bottom line we know enough to respect the rules of Gravitational laws without completely understanding why they exist.
>
> Yet when it comes to heaven and hell we have clearly defined rules, rules that have been known and propagated since the days of the Roman Empire and we object and scream "unfair" to the possibility that choices we make might have consequences that we've already been warned about.

To what really mattered when Moses talked to God:

> Any of those answers and others you might think of are feasible and logical, but as far as Moses was concerned, it didn't matter. All that mattered is that the water appeared as the Lord said it would. The science behind it, and the miracle, whether a miracle of spontaneous creation or simple anticipation is irrelevant, what mattered was the water was there for the people to drink. Moses didn't have to understand the source of the water except that it came from God.

In fact, I had written what could be considered a short version of this book back in **2010 on Marian Prayer.**

Many of these pieces are in the nature of Catholic apologists, and this book is no different but in many ways this book is more of an invitation.

Because when it comes down to it the graces that are available to those who pray either the Hail Mary or the Rosary, in full or in part, are no more dependent on the belief or approval of any particular person or denomination than the existence of God is on people's belief in him.

They are simple facts, and while this book will explain these facts, its ultimate purpose is to convince you to put these facts and these prayers in action, both for the sake of your soul and the sake of other's souls. That's what it's all about.

One final thing, I am a blogger, not a theologian. The only position I have in the Catholic Church is that of a baptized cradle Catholic and the closest thing to formal training I have is seven years of Catholic Grade school and a lifetime of sermons, weekly masses and two years of regular daily mass augmented by reading of scripture and various Catholic apologists in print, online, in Catholic media such as EWTN, various pilgrimages and events where the faith is taught. The language, style and argument you see here will reflect this.

I ask the blessing of the Trinity, God the Father, God the Son and God the Holy Spirit and the patronage of the Blessed Mother, may they use these words for the good of souls and the glory of God.

Introduction

Mrs Mary Cooper: [Walking into a Catholic chapel] Oh, this one's sweet. You know, for your rosary rattlers.

The Big Bang Theory, The Rhinitis Revelation 2011

If there is one thing that tends to unite Protestants of almost every denomination, particularly in America, it's their dislike and or distrust of the Catholic faith. One may go from being a Lutheran, to a Methodist, to a Baptist, to a Congregationalist and it will produce nary a reaction from any other Protestant. But if a Protestant goes from any of these denominations to the Catholic Faith the shockwaves this produces never cease to amaze.

Part of this is of course historical. The country was founded largely (but not exclusively) by Protestants, and religious dissenters whose primary historical enemies were Catholic France and Catholic Spain. Moreover, England had regular issues with Catholic Ireland. Additionally, much of the early immigration to the United States came from Protestant Northern Europe. Furthermore to independent minded people, praying in the vernacular, that elected or hired their own pastors, any church full of strange rituals, full of people saying prayers in Latin (at least till the mid 60's) and ruled by a "foreign prince" (The Pope) was something to distrust.

Of the various Catholic Devotions, none seem to promote more of a visceral reaction than any devotion to Mary. The symbol of that devotion is the Holy Rosary and the primary prayer of the Rosary is the Hail Mary:

Hail Mary, full of grace the Lord is with thee

Blessed art thou amongst women and blessed is the fruit of your womb, Jesus.

Holy Mary, mother of God, pray for us sinners.

Now, and at the hour of our death, Amen.

Nothing seems to set some Protestants into a fit like this prayer. As St. Louis De Montfort described it in his classic book The Secret of the Rosary:

They still say the Our Father, but never the Hail Mary; they would rather wear a poisonous snake around their necks than wear a scapular or carry a rosary.

I've always found this fact to be one of the oddest things about the various Protestant versions of Christianity as the Hail Mary is built in its entirety of words that most Protestants would consider the building blocks of Christianity itself and involve the actions of a person whose faith in God and belief in Christ they do not question in the least.

So this being the feast of **Our Lady of the Rosary** and the Hail Mary being the most common prayer of the rosary (said 10 times in a decade, 53 times if saying one set of mysteries, or 203 times in a full Rosary, 206 using my personal method) this is an excellent time to take a close look at the Hail Mary piece by piece and explain why it is a prayer every Christian, particularly Protestants, should use with pleasure. I will do this in several parts, line by line.

In part 1: *The Angelic Salutation,* we'll talk about how the opening words of the Hail Mary, taken directly from the greeting of the Angel Gabriel as sent by God, signifies not only the importance of Mary as the very first Christian but her position relative to the heavenly host.

In part 2: *The Human Confirmation,* we'll note how the words of Elizabeth's greeting to Mary from scripture not only provides confirmation of the angel's message concerning Mary's status but demonstrates that in addition to the angels it is for man both born and unborn to honor Mary in every generation.

In part 3: *The Holy Name,* we'll discuss not only the power of the Holy Name of Jesus but point out that the Hail Mary is direct worship of Jesus by the invocation of his holy name.

In part 4: *The Maternal Observation,* we'll reflect scripturally on Mary's place as mother of God and disciple of Christ.

In part 5: *The Requested intercession,* we'll note the legitimacy of intercessory prayer, its history in scripture and how Mary's intercession always leads to Christ.

In part 6: *The Timely Intervention,* we'll finish discussing the importance of the intercessory action of Mary when we will need it most.

Finally, we will close with **part 7:** *The Surest Path* where we sum up the whys and wherefores of Marian Prayer in general & the Hail Mary in particular

As might be expected I will be quoting scripture extensively

throughout. All scripture used comes directly from the Vatican

Web Site (http://www.vatican.va/archive/ENG0839/_INDEX.HTM) unless otherwise noted, so that if you have access to the internet, you can confirm the quotes you see. "Whenever God or Jesus is speaking in biblical quotes their words will appear in red."

If you are reading an electronic version of the book you will find some hyperlinks embedded to both scripture and some other items.

This book, while coming from a Catholic perspective, is written for Protestants. If you are a Catholic the arguments that follow will be useful as an informed adult faith is not only the best resistance to those who would try to remove it but is the most likely to bear fruit of the spirit to the betterment of both yourself and others.

Part 1
The Angelic Salutation
"Hail Mary, full of grace, the Lord is with thee."

When we read that the messenger addresses Mary as "full of grace," the Gospel context, which mingles revelations and ancient promises, enables us to understand that among all the "spiritual blessings in Christ" this is a special "blessing." In the mystery of Christ she is present even "before the creation of the world," as the one whom the Father "has chosen" as Mother of his Son in the Incarnation. And, what is more, together with the Father, the Son has chosen her, entrusting her eternally to the Spirit of holiness.

St Pope John Paul II REDEMPTORIS MATER

If one studies various books on the Hail Mary you will see that it is often referred to as the "Angelic Salutation". This makes a whole lot of sense because this prayer begins literally with the salutation of an angel.

Throughout the Bible there are many occasions when angels appear, usually to deliver a message, or perform a specific task. Most angels like the one who frees Peter (Acts 12) are unnamed. It is a rare case where scripture uses one of the three named (Michael, Raphael[1], Gabriel) angels.

As these named angels are rarely seen, the use of named angel to deliver this message to Mary emphasizes its significance. Just as important however to the presence of a named Angel are the actual words being said by Gabriel and what goes on in this encounter with the Virgin Mary. Let's examine it in four parts:

A. **THE SUBSTANCE OF THE ANGEL GABRIEL'S GREETING TO MARY.**

As I've said the Hail Mary or the Angelic Salutation literally begins with the **salutation of Gabriel the Angel:**

> In the sixth month, the angel Gabriel was sent from god to a town of Galilee called Nazareth, to a virgin betrothed to a man named Joseph, of the house of David, and the virgin's name was Mary. And coming to her, he said, "Hail, favored one! The lord is with you."
>
> *Luke 1:26-28*

---

[1] The Angel Raphael appears in the Old Testament Book of Tobit. While part of the Catholic Biblical Canon from the very beginning most Protestants may not have heard of him as their versions of Scripture either omit Tobit altogether or confine it to the apocrypha.

For my protestant friends, here is the King James Version

> And in the sixth month the angel Gabriel was sent from god unto a city of Galilee, named Nazareth, to a virgin espoused to a man whose name was Joseph, of the house of David; and the virgin's name was Mary. And the angel came in unto her, and said, hail, thou that art highly favoured, the lord is with thee: blessed art thou among women.

Now the simple fact that this opening is directly biblical should, make it acceptable to any Christian of any denomination, but the words being said makes this point even better for reasons that will shortly become apparent. Let's examine these words in a way one might normally not, in reverse order.

Gabriel closes his initial words with: "Blessed are thou among women."[2] This singles Mary out from her entire gender as important, but that in itself isn't a big deal. While this puts her above half the earth's population, women were pretty much property at the time so that only suggests she is first among the lowly, the unimportant, but let's continue to go backwards.

---

[2] As the various Catholic Translations do not include Gabriel saying "blessed is the fruit of your womb" we will leave those words aside but if included they would tend, in my opinion, to reinforce the argument made here.

Gabriel precedes this with "THE LORD IS WITH YOU." This echoes the words of the unnamed Angel who greeted Gideon the same way (Judges 6:12) So it establishes her parity with one of the Judges of Israel. That's rather significant particularly since she is a woman and he is a man, but even beyond this while Gideon's angel is unnamed this greeting to Mary is made by Gabriel, a named Angel who stands before God. Thus, Mary is not just equal to the great Judge Gideon, but superior to him in status.

This is preceded by "FAVORED ONE" Now one might think that being visited by an angel alone would make such a statement superfluous, after all who is more favored than a person visited by God's angel? But the explicit statement of this denotes rank, _you_ are favored, _you_ are special, but consider that this is *the only time in the entire bible that this description* is given by an angel to any person. Thus, makes Mary unique, not just above a Judge or the Judges of Israel but above _everyone_, which is pretty much how the Catholic Church views her compared to all other humans other than Christ.

Finally, this entire greeting from Gabriel begins with the formal HAIL, this signifies a person of authority and is usually given by an inferior to a superior. Gabriel having established Mary above humans establishes her above himself.

All of this is entirely in keeping with a Royal Style, a person of rank with multiple titles is addressed by their highest first, and then by their lower ranks and honors in decreasing order.

Thus, Gabriel in that initial salutation immediately establishes Mary's rank, above women, above judges, above creatures and above himself.

B. THE DEFERENCE OF THE ANGEL GABRIEL TO THE VIRGIN MARY

We've just presented our argument that the substance of the Angel Gabriel greeting to Mary establishes her superiority in rank to him. While the case stands well on its own merits it's the contrast between Gabriel's words and actions in her presence vs his previous conversation with Zechariah, the husband of her cousin Elizabeth, that really puts the exclamation mark on Mary's rank in the eternal hierarchy.

Consider the scene in Luke 1:15-17: Zechariah has just been told his prayers have been heard. His elderly wife will conceive by him and his son will have the spirit and power of the prophet Elijah. That' pretty good news for an old priest but an incredible thing to believe so Zechariah quite rationally asks: How?

> Zechariah said to the angel, "how shall I know this? For I am an old man, and my wife is advanced in years." And the angel said to him in reply, "I am Gabriel, who stand before God. I was sent to speak to you and to announce to you this good news. But now you will be speechless and unable to talk until the day these things take place, because you did not believe my words, which will be fulfilled at their proper time."

Luke 1:18-20

Think about this for a second. Zechariah, despite being not only a priest (Luke 1:5) and a man who scripture says was: RIGHTEOUS IN THE EYES OF GOD, OBSERVING ALL THE COMMANDMENTS AND ORDINANCES OF THE LORD BLAMELESSLY (Luke 1:6b) when he responds to Gabriel words with a perfectly rational question:

"How shall I know this?"

He is punished for the full term of his wife's pregnancy for daring to question Gabriel words.

That's a pretty severe chastisement.

Contrast the Angel Gabriel's reaction to Zachariah question vs how he replies to the Virgin Mary who in verse 34 asks:

"How can this be, since I have no relations with a man?"

Are our eyes deceiving us or has Mary just questioned the words of Gabriel, an angel who stands before God? What is his reaction?

- Does Gabriel ask how dare this mere woman question the angel of God?

- Does he note her youth and inexperience and demand she trust him?

- Does he choose to punish this impudent woman in the same why he did the righteous Zachariah?

No.

Not only does Gabriel answer her question directly in verse 35 but in verses 36 and 37 even offers tangible verifiable proof of his assertions concerning the works of God.

> "The Holy Spirit will come upon you, and the power of the most high will overshadow you. Therefore, the child to be born will be called holy, the son of god." And behold, Elizabeth, your relative, has also conceived a son in her old age, and this is the sixth month for her who was called barren; for nothing will be impossible for God."

So, Gabriel, who stands before God, who just six months earlier smote a righteous priest for daring to question him, when standing before a person who in the 1st century had no standing or importance whatsoever, deigns to submit himself to her, providing explanations when asked.

Just like a subordinate would.

C. **THE SUBMISSION OF MARY TO THE WILL OF GOD:**

While all of what has come before is of great importance when considering Mary's status with God, man and the Angelic host, the single most significant clue concerning that relationship and Mary's place in it comes not from the Gabriel's greeting to Mary nor his consenting to answering her questions. It's what follows that elevates Mary beyond everything else.

Consider Mary's position. She has just been told that it is God's intention for her to conceive his son, but Mary being a product of her time and place knows very well where she stands in the pecking order in Jewish society and what turning up pregnant before her wedding means in 1st century Nazareth

1. As an unmarried woman found not only to be pregnant before her wedding, but pregnant not by her betrothed her best case scenario would be a quiet divorce (Which was Joseph's original plan see Matt 1:19) going away for a while, having the baby secretly and giving it up before returning. There would be whispers and rumours that would dissuade any other man from having her. Yet before these rumours she would have to keep silent. After all if she repeated this tale she would be considered a liar, a fool or a blasphemer subject to being stoned to death. Again, <u>this is her best case scenario!</u>

2. Alternatively, after such a divorce the reason for it might come out so instead of rumour her dishonour would become fact. She would be marked as an unclean woman the object of public scorn ridicule and condemnation forcing her to flee elsewhere with the ambition of living our her life as a beggar or a whore to survive.

3. Of course, rather than go through all those potential years of trouble an anguish she might find herself meeting a quicker fate of being publicly denounced as an adulteress and stoned to death according to the law of Moses.

[3]All of these amplified by the mind of a young girl, are the reality of her times, yet given these very real possibilities what does she say:

Mary said, "Behold, I am the handmaid of the Lord. May it be done to me according to your word."

---

3   Now people being people and human nature not really having changed over time, one might assume Mary was not the first Jewish bride to come up pregnant and was not going to be the last so why isn't the possibility of Joseph choosing to marry her on the my list of Mary's considerations? Well the answer is quite simple and might not occur to us with our modern sensibilities. As scripture confirms the virginity of Mary there is no possibility that Joseph might assume the child was his. Thus such a marriage at best would make him the object of gossip at worse if people discover the child is not his, a laughing stock making a decision to marry Mary highly improbable.

Mary in one fell swoop declares her submission to the will of God and displays her trust that God will deliver her from any of those very likely scenarios before her.

Furthermore, her acceptance of Gabriel's words followed by her statement of faith makes an affirmative declaration that she believes the child she will bear, Jesus Christ, is the son of God and by doing so gives birth to Christianity 9 months before the birth of Christ himself, even before his very conception. She becomes by these words the very first Christian.

D. GABRIEL'S DEPARTURE AFTER HER CONSENT

The final piece of this incredible puzzle comes in verse 38b and seems almost not worth mentioning:

"Then the angel departed from her."

I can hear the words now. "Well of course the Angel left her, he's an angel not a midwife or a Lamaze coach." But there are three salient points worth noting here:

1. At the beginning of the sequence in verse 26 Gabriel is referred to by name, but from the moment he proclaims the initial angelic salutation to this final verse, *he is no longer named,* he simply becomes "The Angel" while Mary is continually named each time she speaks.

2. If God considered Mary simple the object to be used to fulfil scripture Gabriel could have easily left after his explanation in verse 37 or even after his basic announcement after verse 33. Instead he waits for her answer. He waits while Mary, a mere creature *decides if God design will take place through her or not.* This act makes Mary's "Yes" not a formality <u>but the necessary final ingredient for God's plan to take place.</u> His waiting for that "yes" is a formal acknowledgement by the powers of heaven in her unique role in the salvation of all of mankind.

3. Finally, consider the words Mary uses to end the conversation. While the substance is completely about submission to the Lord the tone of the text sounds an awful lot like a dismissal of the time a person of authority gives to a subordinate who has asked a favor and has had it granted. In effect Gabriel *does not leave till dismissed.*

4. This gives the final touch to the argument concerning Mary rank vs the Angels

So, in summation in four parts we see Mary:

- Marked as holy by God (part A)

- Submitted to by the heavenly angel (part B & D)

- And giving affirmative consent to god submitting herself to his plan of salvation (part C)

All of this starts with the opening phrases of the Angelic Salutation: "Hail Mary, full of grace, the Lord is with thee."

It is the phrase that all Christianity begins with.

Part 2
The Human Confirmation

"Blessed art thou amongst women and blessed is the fruit of your womb."

Even if you are on the brink of damnation, even if you have one foot in hell, even if you have sold your soul to the devil, as sorcerers do who practice black magic and even if you are a heretic as obstinate as the Devil, sooner or later you will be converted and save your soul if –and mark well what I say–if you say the Rosary every day for the purpose of knowing the truth and obtaining pardon and contrition for your sins.

St Louis De Montfort The Secret of the Rosary

The next words of the Hail Mary are:

> *Blessed art thou amongst women and blessed is the fruit of your womb,*

Like the initial line this comes directly from scripture let's go back to Luke chapter 1 and take this passage in context:

During those days Mary set out and traveled to the hill country in haste to a town of Judah where she entered the house of Zechariah and greeted Elizabeth. When Elizabeth heard Mary's greeting, the infant leaped in her womb, and Elizabeth, filled with the holy spirit, cried out in a loud voice and said,

"most blessed are you among women, and blessed is the fruit of your womb. And how does this happen to me, that the mother of my lord should come to me? For at the moment the sound of your greeting reached my ears, the infant in my womb leaped for joy. Blessed are you who believed that what was spoken to you by the lord would be fulfilled."

Luke 1:39-45

As we did before let's include the King James version:

And Mary arose in those days, and went into the hill country with haste, into a city of Juda; and entered into the house of Zacharias, and saluted Elisabeth. And it came to pass, that, when Elisabeth heard the salutation of Mary, the babe leaped in her womb; and Elisabeth was filled with the holy ghost: and she spake out with a loud voice, and said, blessed art thou among women, and blessed is the fruit of thy womb. And whence is this to me, that the mother of my lord should come to me? For, lo, as soon as the voice of thy salutation sounded in mine ears, the babe leaped in my womb for joy. And blessed is she that believed: for there shall be a performance of those things which were told her from the lord.

As with the angelic greeting not only the words that are part of the Hail Mary but the entire passage is important to understand it. Let's consider it point by point:

A. **THE UNBORN JOHN THE BAPTIST REACTS IN THE WOMB TO MARY'S PHYSICAL PRESENCE.**

Let's begin not with the first reaction of Elizabeth to Mary's greeting, let's begin with the first person who reacts period, the unborn St. John the Baptist in verse 41a:

> *When Elizabeth heard Mary's greeting, the infant leaped in her womb*

Mary is heard and John reacts. This child, who will have the spirit and power of Elijah, reacts to the sound of the Mother of the Christ.

Now one might first say, "Big deal babies jump in the womb all the time.", but let's remind everybody what Gabriel said about John in verse 15:

> *"He will be filled with the Holy Spirit even from his mother's womb,"*

Luke, inspired by the same Holy Spirit that moved John to leap in the womb, considered it important enough to be included in scripture. This means it's *very* significant. That leads to our 2nd point:

B. **THE HOLY SPIRIT REACTS TO THE PRESENCE OF MARY**

The Unborn St. John already filled with the Spirit of Elijah has acted and the next action comes, not from Elizabeth but directly from God in verse 41b:

Elisabeth filled with the Holy Spirit...

At the presence of Mary the Holy Spirit fills Elisabeth. This is quite interesting in that while John apparently already has the spirit of Elijah in him the Holy Spirit does not enter Elisabeth until this point.

So right away we see Mary's greeting causes one already inspired by God to act, and further causes the spirit of God himself to act. It's earth shattering, God acting due to the words of Mary. We'll talk about that in a future chapter.

But even beyond those two things is what happens next our 3rd point:

C. **ELIZABETH PRAISES MARY AND DIRECTLY HONORS HER PRESENCE.**

John and the Holy Spirit have both acted. Now Elizabeth speaks the words that will appear in the Hail Mary:

> *"Most blessed are you among women, and*
> *blessed is the fruit of your womb."*

Now in one sense this simply reiterates what the Angel Gabriel has said already[4] but consider how radical it is. Elisabeth is the elder woman she is married, yet here she is defying all the social and cultural norms by speaking thus to a younger unmarried (and pregnant) relative. By saying these words inspired by the Holy Spirit she is giving confirmation to those words.

Then consider what, under that inspiration of the spirit, comes next.

> *And how does this happen to me, that the*
> *mother of my Lord should come to me?*

Note carefully what she says, she doesn't proclaim herself honored at the presence of her Lord, declares herself honored by the visit of the <u>mother</u> of her Lord.

> *For at the moment the sound of your greeting*
> *reached my ears, the infant in my womb*
> *leaped for joy.*

---

4   As we have already stated in the King James version quoted in Chapter 1 these words are also spoken by Gabriel but the inspiration by the Holy Spirit would confirm these words via God's Spirit itself.

She notes, under the inspiration of the Holy Spirit that it was <u>Mary's</u> voice, which prompted the reaction of her unborn child St. John.

> *"Blessed are you who believed that what was spoken to you by the Lord would be fulfilled."*

And then she finishes her speech by praising Mary for her belief in the Lord's word.

What does all this mean? Just this:

We have already established in Part one that the Angels consider Mary their superior, now here is a woman, who like the Angel before her, would normally be considered of a higher social stature, giving her praise as well.

The symbolism here is striking. Just as the Angel representing the heavenly host elevates Mary above him, both Elizabeth and her child representing all mankind elevates Mary above them. And let's not forget how important the unborn John the Baptist is here. This elevation is of Mary is made both by a generation born and a generation *<u>not yet born</u>*.

Now none of this, of course decreases for one second either the importance or the divinity of the child Jesus, but the example here is profound under the inspiration of God the Holy Spirit mankind, both born and unborn explicitly praises Mary, and does so per her status as the Mother of the Lord God.

And how does Mary react to all of this? She reacts to this with something spectacular dare we say, magnificent.

D. MARY CONFIRMS HER STANDING BEFORE MAN FOR ALL TIME WHILE GIVING GLORY TO GOD

Mary's answers these greetings with her song the prayer we Catholics call the Magnificat:

> "My soul proclaims the greatness of the lord; my spirit rejoices in God my savior. For he has looked upon his handmaid's lowliness; behold, from now on will all ages call me blessed. The mighty one has done great things for me, and Holy is his name. His mercy is from age to age to those who fear him. He has shown might with his arm, dispersed the arrogant of mind and heart. He has thrown down the rulers from their thrones but lifted up the lowly. The hungry he has filled with good things; the rich he has sent away empty. He has helped Israel his servant, remembering his mercy, according to his promise to our fathers, to Abraham and to his descendants forever."
>
> *Luke 1:46b-55*

Look at what Mary does here: she *"Proclaims the greatness of the Lord"* proclaims *"God her savior"*, notes the holiness of his name, his mercy and talks of his great deeds and promises, but in the middle of all this praise she also confirms that:

"From now on will all ages call me blessed"

This coincidentally is exactly what this line of the Hail Mary does.

There's one more thing about Mary's speech worth noting here. While Luke explicitly stated that Elizabeth words are inspired by the Holy Spirit when she reacts to Mary inspired scripture doesn't say anything about the Holy Spirit inspiring Mary prayer or speech in any way.

That's extremely significant particularly when you consider that the in the very next passage when Luke tells the story of the birth and naming of John the Baptist (Luke 1 57-80) and the Cantle of Zachariah is proclaimed (verses 68-79) once again the inspiration of the Holy Spirit is explicitly stated by Luke.

Given its exclusion here we must conclude that at this point Mary is already so advanced in grace and so blessed that she properly praises God without the need of further inspiration. The irony of course is while Mary may not need the spirits inspiration to praise God it's significant that the spirit inspires Luke to record it.

Lets' review:

- Mary's words cause a reaction by the great St. John (A)

- Mary's words cause the Holy Spirit to enter Elizabeth (B)

- Elizabeth praises Mary under the inspiration of god (C)

- Mary confirms this praise is proper while at the same time praising God as well. (D)

This says that Mary is not only to be praised by man, both those born and those yet to come, but it is to happen for all generations.

All of this all of this comes from inspired scripture, scripture that is not in dispute between Protestants and Catholics.

One final thought, you will note that I have spent almost the entire chapter on the first half of this line. "Blessed art thou among woman" & almost nothing on the words "Blessed is the fruit of your womb."

That is not an accident. The target audience of this book is our fellow Christians all of which bring their own flavor to their worship of God and their devotion to Christ, and these disagreements both between Catholics and Protestants and between various Protestant denominations have been the source of division, debate and even violence on occasion.

If there is one thing that every one of us agree on, if there is one thing that not even one of us who claim the label Christian would dispute is this:

The fruit of Mary womb, the Christ the son of the living God, our savior and redeemer is very blessed indeed.

But for the sake of those who might come from a different faith tradition or no faith at all let's include two verses to confirm this contention:

> Now there were shepherds in that region living in the fields and keeping the night watch over their flock. The angel of the Lord appeared to them and the Glory of the Lord shone around them, and they were struck with great fear.
>
> The angel said to them, "Do not be afraid; for behold, I proclaim to you good news of great joy that will be for all the people. For today in the city of David a savior has been born for you who is messiah and lord.
>
> And this will be a sign for you: you will find an infant wrapped in swaddling clothes and lying in a manger." and suddenly there was a multitude of the heavenly host with the angel, praising god and saying: glory to god in the highest and on earth peace to those on whom his favor rests."
>
> *Luke 2:8-14*

Thus, the Angelic Host confirms who Jesus is but on his day of circumcision their testimony is augmented by a man named Simeon:

> Now there was a man in Jerusalem whose name was Simeon. This man was righteous and devout, awaiting the consolation of Israel, and the Holy Spirit was upon him. It had been revealed to him by the Holy Spirit that he should not see death before he had seen the messiah of the lord.

He came in the spirit into the temple; and when the parents brought in the child Jesus to perform the custom of the law in regard to him, he took him into his arms and blessed god, saying:

"Now, master, you may let your servant go in peace, according to your word. For my eyes have seen your salvation, which you prepared in sight of all the peoples, a light for revelation to the gentiles, and glory for your people Israel."

Luke 2:25-32

We have the testimony both inside the womb of the Angel Gabriel, and Elizabeth inspired by the Holy Spirit. Outside the Womb we have the Angelic Host and Simeon also inspired by the spirit.

From that testimony, we can safely conclude that the fruit of Mary's womb is indeed, blessed.

Part 3
The Holy Name:
Jesus!

Love is never monotonous in the uniformity of its expression. The mind is infinitely variable in its language, but the heart is not. The heart of a man, in the face of the woman he loves, is too poor to translate the infinity of his affection into a different word. So the heart takes one expression, "I love you," and in saying it over and over again, it never repeats. It is the only real news in the universe. That is what we do when we say the rosary, we are saying to god, the trinity, to the incarnate saviour, to the blessed mother: "I love you, I love you, I love you."

Venerable Fulton Sheen

It might seem odd to give a full chapter to a single word in a prayer but it is the single most important word out there.

Jesus.

There are three important things to consider concerning the use of "Jesus" in the Hail Mary prayer.

A. HOW THE HOLY NAME "JESUS" AFFECTS THE HAIL MARY'S STRUCTURE.

There are several functions that the name of Jesus gives to the structure of the Hail Mary.

1. The use of Jesus here delineates and unites the two parts of the prayer, the scriptural sections which establish the place of Mary which we've already discussed at the beginning of the prayer and the intercessory sections, which are yet to come, are where we make the primary requests in this prayer.

2. The use of Jesus here completes the previous phrase reminding us of Mary's status, and the primary reason of Mary's favour was that she had been declared, by the grace of God, worthy to bear the Messiah and accepted that charge.

3. It emphasizes the humanity of Christ, not simply the fruit of the Spirit, but the fruit of a human womb. He is the son of a mother, which we will explore in the next two sections of this book.

It is the syllable emphasized within the prayer, the key moment. Any person who has watched someone praying the Hail Mary sees that when the person says the word "Jesus" it is an emphasized word.

It is this emphasis that establishes Jesus as both the object and the target of worship being conducted within the prayer. The emphasis is on Jesus, which makes this prayer explicitly Christian.

This leads, of course, to the second thing to consider.

B. THE POWER OF HOLY NAME OF JESUS IN THE HAIL MARY

One cannot overstate the power and importance of the name of Jesus.

- Remember it was by the name of Jesus that Peter healed the **cripple at the gate. (Acts 3)**

- It was by the name of Jesus that the building shook and **the Holy Spirit came upon them again. (Acts 4)**

- It was by the **proclamation of Jesus that the Ethiopian was converted. (Acts 8)**

- It was in the name of **Jesus Christ that the first gentiles were baptised. (Acts 10)**

- The Name of **Jesus is the profession that Paul speaks of to the Romans. (Romans 10)**

- It is the location of Truth as he tells the **Ephesians. (Ephesians 4)**

- It is the name of Jesus that **John says we should believe in. (1 John 3)** and warns us **not to deny (1 John 2)** and is the **test of spirits** John warns us not to deny. **(1 John 4)**

- It is Jesus who Paul tell Timothy will judge the **living & dead. (2 Timothy 4)**

- It is by the name of Jesus that Paul tells the Corinthians **they are justified (1 Corinthians 6)** and later tells them, in a verse worth quoting in full

> No one can say, "**Jesus** is **lord**," except by the **Holy Spirit**
>
> *1 Corinthians 12:3b*

And that he, in another verse worth quoting in full, tells **the Philippians:**

> At the name of Jesus every knee should bend, of those in heaven and on earth and under the earth, and every tongue confess that Jesus Christ is Lord, to the glory of God the Father.
>
> *Philippians 2:10-11*

Those are just the biblical references. We could turn to the saints, the fathers of the church and Bishops and Popes for centuries preaching the power of and in the name of Jesus (not to mention plenty of post reformation Protestant sources as well) but if I tried to search for them all I would die of old age before I even began. I will settle for this from St. John Vianney the patron of parish priests:

> *With the name of Jesus we shall overthrow the demons; we shall put them to flight. With this name, if they sometimes dare to attack us, our battles will be victories, and our victories will be crowns for heaven, all brilliant with precious stones.*

There is nothing more powerful than the name of Jesus and that leads to a perspective that most people don't see or forget concerning the Hail Mary.

C. **THE HAIL MARY AS DIRECT WORSHIP OF CHRIST THROUGH HIS HOLY NAME.**

The Lord's Prayer (or as it is colloquially known, the "Our Father") which was given to us directly by Christ is of course the most excellent of prayers. It is the primary prayer spoken by Christians from the very start of Christianity, prayed at every single Catholic mass and said at the start of every single decade of the Rosary. In fact, you would be hard pressed to find any Catholic devotion that does not include at least one "Our Father" in it.

But if you look at the Our Father there is one thing you might notice…

…the name of Jesus is not mentioned in it.

This is, in one sense, not a surprise; Jesus gave the disciples this prayer during his ministry at a time when the Disciples still did not understand his nature completely. While eventually they perceived that Jesus was the Son of God it's unclear that they understood at that time Jesus taught them that prayer that Jesus was God himself. It is no coincidence that it isn't until after Christ's resurrection that we hear these words from one of the disciples:

> Now a week later his disciples were again inside and Thomas was with them. Jesus came, although the doors were locked, and stood in their midst and said, "Peace be with you." Then he said to Thomas, "Put your finger here and see my hands, and bring your hand and put it into my side, and do not be unbelieving, but believe."
>
> Thomas answered and said to him, My Lord and my God!" Jesus said to him, "Have you come to believe because you have seen me? Blessed are those who have not seen and have believed."
>
> John 20:26-29

Now consider, in contrast, the Hail Mary, every single time you pray the Hail Mary you are <u>*saying*</u> and <u>*praying*</u> the Holy Name of Jesus.

That's a powerful thing, but it gets better.

The Hail Mary is the primary prayer of the Holy Rosary so for every decade of the Rosary you say, you are praying the holy name of Jesus 10 times (11 if you pray the Fatima prayer at the end of the decade which goes: <u>"oh my Jesus forgive us our sins, save us from the fires of hell and lead us all into heaven especially those in most need of thy mercy.)</u>

It also means every full set of Mysteries with the intro & the Hail Holy Queen at the end you are saying and praying the Holy name of Jesus 55 times (60 with the Fatima prayer)

And of course, it means if you pray the full 20 decades of the Rosary with the intro and the Fatima prayer you have invoked and pray the holy name of Jesus **228 times**. It's no wonder that the famous 20th Century Saint Padre Pio said this about the Rosary:

> *"The Rosary is the weapon given us by Mary to use against the tricks of the infernal enemy."*

Now there are those who critique repetitive prayer but no matter what brand of Christianity you proclaim we can all agree that you can't go wrong repeating the Holy Name of Jesus.

And if you are praying the Hail Mary that most Catholic of prayers, that's exactly what you're doing.

Part 4
The Maternal Observation

"Holy Mary, mother of God,"

God the father gave his only son to the world only through Mary. Whatever desires the patriarchs may have cherished, whatever entreaties the prophets and saints of the old law may have had for 4,000 years to obtain that treasure, it was Mary alone who merited it and found grace before god by the power of her prayers and the perfection of her virtues. "the world being unworthy," said Saint Augustine, "to receive the Son of God directly from the hands of the father, he gave his son to Mary for the world to receive him from her."

St. Louis de Montfort <u>True Devotion to Mary</u>

As we have just finished the first half of the Hail Mary it's a good point to take stock at where we are.

In reviewing the Hail Mary we've discussed the greeting of **the Angelic Salutation**, establishing the importance of Mary, in **the Human confirmation,** we noted how Elizabeth's greeting confirmation that importance for all time while in **The Holy Name:** We noted both the power of the Holy Name of Jesus & Hail Mary as direct worship of Jesus Christ.

Up to this point each phrase of the Hail Mary that we discussed was either directly quoting scripture or invoking the Holy Name of Jesus. That being the case our Protestant brothers would not, indeed could not object to them as false, or improper without a direct critique of scripture or of the Holy name of Jesus, making our task of explaining the Hail Mary to our protestant brother fairly easy.

We have however reached the point in the prayer where the text of the Hail Mary is no longer directly lifted from inspired scripture; therefore, from the perspective of explaining the Hail Mary to our Protestant brothers, it will be necessary to examine the rest of the prayer from two perspectives:

A. **WE NEED TO CONFIRM THE WORDS ARE TRUE & PROPER**

If as a Catholic I wish my brother Christians to even consider my case for the Hail Mary, it's necessary to confirm for them that any statement made in the prayer from this point is a statement of absolute fact. Furthermore if rather than a statement, a request or petition is made, it must be confirmed that the petition is consistent with proper Christian Practice.

Then once the veracity of the statement or the properness of the petition is established we can return to the task performed in the previous three chapters when evaluating the prayer

B. **EXPLAINING THE SIGNIFICANCE OF PRAYING THESE WORDS**

So, with our two tasks firmly in mind let's begin by performing the primary task of examining the words in question and establish them as facts:

Holy Mary, mother of God,

Let's start with the words "Holy Mary".

A. **Mary is Holy because the followers of Christ are Holy.**

We've already by examining the words of the Angel Gabriel, established that Mary is the first of the believers, the very first Christian, who consented to God plan at risk to herself (Luke 1:26-38) who stood by Christ at his crucifixion when all the disciples other than John fled (John 19:25-27) and who was present with the Disciples devoted to prayer after the ascension (Acts 1:14). Thus we can firmly establish by scripture itself that Mary was a follower of Christ.

Having established Mary as a believer we can now demonstrate that the description of her as Holy is completely consistent with the New Testament treatment of believers.

In Old Testament with minor exceptions such as Elisha "Holy" is used to describe places or things, Holy Mountains, Holy Bread etc etc but in the New Testament it's made very clear that the believers in Christ are in fact Holy. This is stated by Luke:

> Peter sent them all out and knelt down and prayed. Then he turned to her body and said, "Tabitha, rise up." She opened her eyes, saw Peter, and sat up.
>
> He gave her his hand and raised her up, and when he had called the holy ones and the widows, he presented her alive.
>
> *Acts 9:40-41*

By Paul:

> Contribute to the needs of the Holy ones, exercise hospitality.

By Jude:

> Beloved, although I was making every effort to write to you about our common salvation, i now feel a need to write to encourage you to contend for the faith that was once for all handed down to the Holy ones.
>
> *Jude 3*

By Peter:

> Like obedient children, do not act in compliance with the desires of your former ignorance but, as he who called you is Holy, be holy yourselves in every aspect of your conduct.
>
> *1 Peter 1:14-15*

And by John:

> When he took it, the four living creatures and the twenty-four elders fell down before the lamb. Each of the elders held a harp and gold bowls filled with incense, which are the prayers of the Holy ones.
>
> *Revelation 5:8*

Over and over these New Testament writers in inspired scripture refer to the believers as Holy Ones, even in prophesy. Therefore we have clearly established by inspired scripture that the followers of Christ are the Holy Ones and thus we can state without question:

- **Mary is a follower of Christ.**

- **Scripture repeatedly establishes that the followers of Christ are Holy.**

- **Therefore, the words "Holy Mary" are entirely true and accurate description of her.**

Now let's consider the accuracy of rest of the phrase: "Mother of God"

B. MARY IS THE MOTHER OF GOD BECAUSE SCRIPTURE CLEARLY ESTABLISHES JESUS IS IN FACT GOD.

In his book True Devotion to Mary St. Louis De Montfort, one of the greatest of Marian saints was very clear on Mary's relationship to God the Father

> With the whole church I acknowledge that Mary, being a mere creature fashioned by the hands of god is, compared to his infinite majesty, less than an atom, or rather is simply nothing, since he alone can say, "I am he who is". Consequently, this great Lord, who is ever independent and self-sufficient, never had and does not now have any absolute need of the blessed virgin for the accomplishment of his will and the manifestation of his glory. To do all things he has only to will them.
>
> *True Devotion to Mary: 14*

Yet he along with the entire Catholic, Orthodox and some Protestants (Anglicans & Lutherans) also declare Mary the Mother of God, why?

It is of course no problem to establish Mary as the mother of Christ, Her conception (Luke 1:38) her pregnancy (Luke 1:39-45) her delivery (Luke 2:4-7) and even her admonishing him as a mother does (Luke 2:48) are all clearly established in scripture. But does that mean she can properly be called the Mother of God? Well that depends on one thing: ***<u>Was Jesus in fact God?</u>***

The Heresy that Jesus is lesser than God is called Arianism and was condemned by both the Councils of Nicaea (325 AD) & Constantinople (381 AD) furthermore the term *Theotokos* (Mother of God) to describe Mary dates are far back as he 2nd century and was confirmed at the Council of Ephesus (431 AD) but as our Protestant brothers likely give little weight to any Church Councils after the Council of Jerusalem (approx 50 AD) mentioned in Acts, even ones as early as the 3rd century. So in order to satisfy our Protestant brothers & make our case let's go straight to scripture to the Gospel of John where the question of Christ's divinity is given very clearly right at the start:

> In the beginning was the word, and the word was with god, and the word was god. He was in the beginning with god. All things came to be through him, and without him nothing came to be. What came to be through him was life, and this life was the light of the human race; the light shines in the darkness, and the darkness has not overcome it.
>
> *John 1:1-5*

Thus, we establish that the Word was there at the very beginning and was God from the very start, the light of the Human Race but let's make sure that the light and the word are the same thing.

> A man named John was sent from God. He came for testimony, to testify to the light, so that all might believe through him.
>
> *John 1:6-7*

This verse establishes John the Baptist as opposed to the author John the Apostle, is testifying to the light, which is the word and starting in verse 14 we see the key

> And the word became flesh and made his dwelling among us, and we saw his glory, the glory as of the father's only son, full of grace and truth.
>
> *John 1:14*

So the Word is made flesh, but *who is this word?*

There is a reason why these first 14 verses of John were read of the end of every mass before Vatican 2 and every Latin Mass since, it is the basis of Christian belief that the word was made flesh, *but who is the word?* Two later verses from chapter 1 answer this question.

> John testified to him and cried out, saying, "This was he of whom I said, 'the one who is coming after me ranks ahead of me because he existed before me.
>
> *John 1:15*

John did so again later in the chapter:

> The next day he saw Jesus coming toward him and said, "Behold, The Lamb of God, who takes away the sin of the world. He is the one of whom I said, 'A man is coming after me who ranks ahead of me because he existed before me.'
>
> *John 1:29-30*

So John the Baptist testifies to the light as Jesus and also clearly states that Jesus preceded him even though he was conceived before him.

And of course if this isn't enough evidence we can see in John 5:17, 8:24, 8:28, 8:58 Jesus refers to himself directly as the I AM.

In my opinion the clincher comes in his final discourse when he reminds Phillip of what he has seen:

> Philip said to him, "Master, show us the father, and that will be enough for us."
>
> Jesus said to him, "Have I been with you for so long a time and you still do not know me, Philip? Whoever has seen me has seen the Father. How can you say, 'show us the Father'?"
>
> *John 13:8-9*

And of course, after his resurrection when he appears to the Disciples and shows himself to his doubting disciple, Thomas exclaims: "My Lord and my God!" (John 20:28b)

Thus, we clearly established through the Apostle John's writings, through John the Baptist's declaration, through Jesus' words to the people, through his declaration to Philip and through Thomas' confession that he Jesus is in fact God.

So let's review:

- Mary is the Mother of Jesus
- Jesus is in fact God
- Therefore Mary, as Jesus mother, is accurately described as the Mother of God

Thus, we establish that while we are not suggesting in the slightest that Mary preceded God, we affirm through the sacred mystery of Christ as True God & Man that Mary is properly described as the Mother of God.

But now that we've established the facts of the phrase: Holy Mary Mother of God, we still haven't established its purpose, why are we praying it?

Let's think of what we are saying with that phrase.

C. MARY HAS A UNIQUE RELATIONSHIP WITH GOD BEYOND MERELY A BELIEVER.

One might ask why we are establishing highlighting Mary given this famous Gospel exchange emphasizing not the family connection but holiness that makes on blessed

> While he was speaking, a woman from the crowd called out and said to him, "Blessed is the womb that carried you and the breasts at which you nursed." He replied, "Rather, blessed are those who hear the word of god and observe it."
>
> *Luke 11:27-28*

One might think that Catholics, steeped In Mariology might dodge this Gospel, instead it is regularly proclaimed at vigil masses of Marian feasts. It is one of the shortest if not the shortest Gospel reading during the entire Church Calendar but ironically, while that establishes obedience over family connection, it turns out that description accurately describes Mary who heard the word of God proclaimed to her by an angel and kept it. In fact, Christ is almost mimicking Gabriel in this proclamation concerning the blessed.

Thus, we are reinforcing Jesus when we proclaim the holiness of Mary, someone who is holy she and worthy of respect. But the greeting of the Angel and the proclamation that all generations will call her "Blessed" signifies her uniqueness beyond this. Yes Mary is holy but by invoking Mary as the Mother of God we proclaim her far beyond other holy followers of Christ. How far? Consider this:

We've already noted that Jesus is human, the word made flesh, and as a human prayed to God the father even though he himself was God. Over and over the bible references Jesus praying. This is in obedience to the very first commandment as described by Jesus:

> "Teacher, which commandment in the law is the greatest?"
>
> He said to him, "You shall love the lord, your god, with all your heart, with all your soul, and with all your mind.
>
> This is the greatest and the first commandment."
>
> Matthew 22:36-38

Despite being fully God and fully man Jesus by offering prayers to God the father is acting in obedience to the commandment, but as a person Jesus prayer to God is also obedience to another commandment:

> Honor your Father & your Mother.
>
> Exodus 20:12a

So the Jesus by his prayers is loving God as per one commandment and also honors his father per another. But if we see Jesus honoring his father, through prayer where can we see an example of Jesus honoring his mother? Well that's actually pretty easy, we can just go straight to the 2nd Chapter of John:

> On the third day there was a wedding in Cana in Galilee, and the mother of Jesus was there. Jesus and his disciples were also invited to the wedding.

When the wine ran short, the mother of Jesus said to him, "They have no wine." (and) Jesus said to her, "Woman, how does your concern affect me? My hour has not yet come."

His mother said to the servers, "do whatever he tells you."

Now there were six stone water jars there for Jewish ceremonial washings, each holding twenty to thirty gallons.

Jesus told them, "Fill the jars with water." So they filled them to the brim. Then he told them, "Draw some out now and take it to the headwaiter." So they took it. And when the headwaiter tasted the water that had become wine, without knowing where it came from (although the servers who had drawn the water knew)

John 2:1-9b

There are three significant things here concerning this passage. We'll save the 2nd & 3rd for Part 5, but the first is most important and cannot be overemphasized. When Mary approaches Jesus concerning the situation at the wedding, he is most emphatic about it:

"Woman, how does your concern affect me? My hour has not yet come."

Christ clearly and distinctly tells his mother in no uncertain terms that not only is this matter none of his business but that this is not the time for him to take any public action as the messiah. Yet when Mary tells the servers: "Do whatever he tells you" what does Jesus do?

- Does he ignore the situation completely?
- Does her rebuke her because it's not her time?
- Does he dismiss the servers awaiting his command?

No he <u>acts!</u>

The question is why? He doesn't perform a public miracle, only his mother and the servers know what happened, in fact it's not even clear that the disciples know what's going on.

So why does he do it?

I submit and suggest it's because he is acting according to the commandment, he is honoring his mother. There is something that matters to his mother and he acts accordingly. He is acknowledging by this act that his relationship with her is different that his relationship with every single other human who has or will ever exist.

So, let's review, what are we doing when we say: "Holy Mary Mother of God"?

- We are affirming a truth backed up by scripture
- We are invoking both Mary's relationship to Christ as a disciple and as the mother of god backed up by scripture.

And both of these invocations are critical for what will follow.

Part 5
The Requested Intercession

Pray for us sinners.

Is anyone among you suffering? He should pray. Is anyone in good spirits? He should sing praise. Is anyone among you sick? He should summon the presbyters of the church, and they should pray over him and anoint (him) with oil in the name of the lord, and the prayer of faith will save the sick person, and the Lord will raise him up. If he has committed any sins, he will be forgiven. Therefore, confess your sins to one another and pray for one another, that you may be healed. The fervent prayer of a righteous person is very powerful.

James 5:13-16

As per Part four, our task when examining the words "Pray for us sinners" is two-fold, to confirm that these words are true and proper, followed by giving a reason why these words should, in fact, be prayed.

At first glance this would seem rather easy; "Pray for us sinners" would seem an innocuous term. We are of course all sinners who need prayer and any look at a Bible concordance will find the word "pray" and "prayer" all over the place in scripture.

But there is one catch to this that I've heard from just about every sort of Protestant that I've met. It's an argument that is so common I doubt there is a Catholic who prays the Hail Mary who hasn't heard it. It's the idea that you should go directly to Christ with your prayer rather than asking Mary to pray for you. Why would one ask for Mary to intercede when you can pray directly to Jesus Christ? The argument suggests that such prayer raises Mary beyond her station and in some way lessons Christ.

A look at scripture leads however to the following point

A. **INTERCESSORY PRAYER IS NOT ONLY LEGITIMATE BUT BIBLICAL**

This might shock some people, but if you look at scripture it should not. The standard of going directly to God is not always used. There is a hint of this in Jesus Last Supper discourse when he prays during his discourse at the Last Supper (emphasis mine)

> "I pray not only for them, but also for those <u>who will believe in me through their word</u>, so that they may all be one, as you, father, are in me and i in you, that they also may be in us, that the world may believe that you sent me."
>
> John 17:20-21

This indicates the task of the Disciples of Christ and that those who follow after him will have a key impact in the faith and belief in others, in other words that they will intercede on their behalf. But that's only an oblique reference, if you look in scripture you will find examples of this both in the Old Testament where Pharaoh asks Moses to intercede in prayer:

> Then Pharaoh summoned Moses and Aaron and said, "Pray the Lord to remove the frogs from me and my subjects, and I will let the people go to offer sacrifice to the Lord."
>
> Moses answered pharaoh, "Do me the favor of appointing the time when I am to pray for you and your servants and your subjects, that the frogs may be taken away from you and your houses and be left only in the river."
>
> *Exodus 8:4-5*

> Well, then," said Pharaoh, "I will let you go to offer sacrifice to the Lord, your God, in the desert, provided that you do not go too far away and that you pray for me."
>
> Moses answered, "as soon as i leave your presence I will pray to the lord that the flies may depart tomorrow from pharaoh and his servants and his subjects. Pharaoh, however, must not play false again by refusing to let the people go to offer sacrifice to the lord."

When Moses left Pharaoh's presence, he prayed to the Lord; and the Lord did as Moses had asked. He removed the flies from Pharaoh and his servants and subjects. Not one remained.

Exodus 8:24-27

What is Pharaoh doing? *He is asking Moses for intercessory prayer.*

Now some might argue that Pharaoh, not being Hebrew, is of course, asking Moses to pray since the Lord is Moses god not his. The problem with that argument is Pharaoh is not alone in the Old Testament in asking for intercessory prayer.

You have the people of Israel asking it **of Samuel:**

> They said to Samuel, "Pray to the Lord your God for us, your servants, that we may not die for having added to all our other sins the evil of asking for a king."
>
> *1 Samuel 12:19*

The Elder Uzziah asks it **of Judith**

> Then Uzziah said to her: "All that you have said was spoken with good sense, and no one can gainsay your words. Not today only is your wisdom made evident, but from your earliest years all the people have recognized your prudence, which corresponds to the worthy dispositions of your heart.

> The people, however, were so tortured with thirst that they forced us to speak to them as we did, and to bind ourselves by an oath that we cannot break. But now, god-fearing woman that you are, pray for us that the lord may send rain to fill up our cisterns, lest we be weakened still further."
>
> *Judith 8:28-31*

And even the Lord God himself commands it of the **friends of Job**

> And it came to pass after the Lord had spoken these words to job, that the Lord said to Eliphaz the Temanite, "I am angry with you and with your two friends; for you have not spoken rightly concerning me, as has my servant Job.
>
> Now, therefore, take seven bullocks and seven rams, and go to my servant job, and offer up a holocaust for yourselves; and let my servant job pray for you; for his prayer I will accept, not to punish you severely. For you have not spoken rightly concerning me, as has my servant Job."
>
> Then Eliphaz the Temanite, and Bildad the Shuhite, and Zophar the Naamathite, went and did as the Lord had commanded them. And the lord accepted the intercession of job.
>
> *Job 42:7-9*

That final example is very significant because we have an example of God himself ordering Eliphaz, Bildad and Zophar to ask Job to offer intercessory prayer.

Of course, that is all in the Old Testament before the coming of Jesus Christ the intercessor between man and God the father but it turns out intercessory prayer isn't limited to the Old Testament In the new we see Simon the magician's **plea to Peter...**

> Repent of this wickedness of yours and pray to the Lord that, if possible, your intention may be forgiven. For I see that you are filled with bitter gall and are in the bonds of iniquity."
>
> Simon said in reply, "Pray for me to the lord, that nothing of what you have said may come upon me."
>
> *Acts 8:22-24*

...and Paul asking the **Thessalonians**...

> Finally, brothers, pray for us, so that the word of the lord may speed forward and be glorified, as it did among you, and that we may be delivered from perverse and wicked people, for not all have faith.
>
> *2 Thessalonians 3:1-2*

...The Colossians

> Persevere in prayer, being watchful in it with thanksgiving; at the same time, pray for us, too, that God may open a door to us for the word, to speak of the mystery of Christ, for which I am in prison,
>
> *Colossians 4:2-3*

...and the Ephesians

> With all prayer and supplication, pray at every opportunity in the spirit. To that end, be watchful with all perseverance and supplication for all the holy ones and also for me, that speech may be given me to open my mouth, to make known with boldness the mystery of the gospel for which I am an ambassador in chains, so that I may have the courage to speak as I must.
>
> *Ephesians 18-20*

…to pray for him.

All of these things are requests for intercessory prayer, a request that a person other than themselves intercede with God.

Now of course there is nothing wrong with a prayer directed toward Christ and if you have been to a Catholic Mass you would see that it's the norm, in fact will note that just about every opening prayer at every Catholic Mass. ends with some variation of:

> *"..We ask this through Jesus Christ your son, who lives and reigns with you and the Holy Spirit, one God forever and ever. Amen."*

But as we already noted, when Christ teaches the disciples how to pray in both the Gospel of Matthew:

> "This is how you are to pray: Our father in heaven, hallowed be your name, your kingdom come, your will be done, on earth as in heaven. Give us today our daily bread; and forgive us our debts, as we forgive our debtors; and do not subject us to the final test, but deliver us from the evil one.
>
> *Matt 11:9-13*

And the **Gospel of Luke**

> He said to them, "When you pray, say: Father, hallowed be your name, your kingdom come. Give us each day our daily bread and forgive us our sins for we ourselves forgive everyone in debt to us, and do not subject us to the final test."
>
> *Luke 11:2-4*

Jesus, in teaching them the base prayer of Christianity, does not teach them to pray to the Father *through* him, rather he directs that they pray directly to the father.

Now we've already touched on the reason why this might be the case, but what's significant here is while he teaches them to pray directly to the father Christ also tells his Apostles in John's Gospel to ask things of the father in his name:

> On that day you will not question me about anything. Amen, amen, I say to you, whatever you ask the Father in my name he will give you. Until now you have not asked anything in my name; ask and you will receive, so that your joy may be complete. "I have told you this in figures of speech. The hour is coming when I will no longer speak to you in figures but I will tell you clearly about the father. On that day you will ask in my name, and I do not tell you that I will ask the Father for you.
>
> *John 16:23-26*

Yet this statement does not give any modification to the prayer that Christ gave bypassing him, nor will you find such a statement anywhere in scripture.

What does this mean? It means in scripture when it comes to prayer we have a lack of exclusivity. Paul's request for the people to pray for him doesn't exclude his praying to God himself any more than his prayers for them exclude it. Likewise the prayer of the Our Father doesn't exclude prayer in Jesus name or vice versa. Nor do the prayer requests in the Old Testament suggest that the people making these requests are not to pray as well.

In other words <u>all these type of prayer are legitimate.</u> The prayer directly to the Father is legitimate, the prayer in the name of Jesus is legitimate and the prayer for another is legitimate.

Ironically turning back to the Hail Mary we see that in this one prayer there are examples of All three types:

- In the words: "The Lord is with thee" we invoke God the Father.

- In the words: "Blessed is the fruit of your womb Jesus" we invoke Jesus Christ & proclaim his holy name

- And now in the words: "Pray for us sinners" we seek intercessory prayer.

So in the Hail Mary we find ourselves asking of Mary the Mother of God the very same intercessory prayer that we often ask of one another.

This is not only keeping with the precedent of scripture but is consistent with the history of Christianity from its very start as evidenced in the Letter of James that we quoted at the beginning of this Chapter.

> Therefore, confess your sins to one another and pray for one another, that you may be healed. The fervent prayer of a righteous person is very powerful.
>
> *James 5:16*

Thus we have established through examples of Scripture that intercessory prayer has a long history and is a perfectly proper application of the worship of God.

Having established that intercessory prayer is not a problem we can now tackle the 2nd question:

B. WHY MAKE THE INTERCESSION TO "PRAY FOR US SINNERS" THROUGH MARY IN PARTICULAR AND DOES SUCH INTERCESSION ELEVATE HER BEYOND HER PLACE OR DECREASE CHRIST IN ANY WAY?"

There are two points to make here. First of all consider again the examples above from the Old Testament and even the example of Simon that we just examined. In each of them the person who is asked to pray is considered a holy person, one close to God, and Mary, as we already established in Part one, was marked by God as such a person, one who angels themselves deferred to.

God has already elevated her, thus no amount of intercessory prayer offered though her can top that.

But beyond this it's the second point, concerning the story of the Wedding at Cana that we alluded to in the last chapter that really seals the deal on Mary as an intercessor. Let's repeat the passage so you don't have to turn back:

> On the third day there was a wedding in Cana in Galilee, and the mother of Jesus was there. Jesus and his disciples were also invited to the wedding.
>
> When the wine ran short, the mother of Jesus said to him, "they have no wine." (and) Jesus said to her, "Woman, how does your concern affect me? My hour has not yet come."
>
> His mother said to the servers, "Do whatever he tells you."

Now there were six stone water jars there for Jewish ceremonial washings, each holding twenty to thirty gallons.

Jesus told them, "Fill the jars with water." So they filled them to the brim. Then he told them, "Draw some out now and take it to the headwaiter." So they took it. And when the headwaiter tasted the water that had become wine, without knowing where it came from (although the servers who had drawn the water knew) the headwaiter called the bridegroom and said to him, "everyone serves good wine first, and then when people have drunk freely, an inferior one; but you have kept the good wine until now."

Jesus did this as the beginning of his signs in Cana in Galilee and so revealed his glory, and his disciples began to believe in him.

John 2:1-11

We're already dealt with the first significant bit from this passage, Jesus acting in obedience to the commandment to Honor thy father and mother in the previous part. Let's address the next two points of this story

2. Mary humbly places the matter before Christ

We see that in verse 3 Mary tells Jesus of the problem, in verse 4 Jesus plainly notes that this is really not his business, so how does Mary react: She says to the servers, "Do whatever he tells you."

What is important about this answer firstly is what she doesn't say to her son:

- She doesn't play the "Honor thy father & thy mother" card.

- She doesn't press upon him the embarrassment of the couple and plead their case.

- She doesn't note her importance before God already established by an angel & the Holy Spirit.

- She doesn't insist in any way the he do what she asks.

- She does not hint in any way that she might be embarrassed, or sad or disappointed if he does nothing after she has spoken up to others.

No, she simply places her petition on behalf of the happy couple at the feet of the Word Incarnate, entrusts them to his will and instructs the servers to obey that will.

Mary is not God, nor has she been assumed to heaven yet. She has not been given the gift of prophecy and she is years away from the gifts of the spirit that will come on Pentecost Sunday. She doesn't know if Jesus will choose to act, she doesn't know if he will choose not to act, she is content to have her request subject to his design and asks us to obey.

That is a perfect example of the Humility of Mary in her intercession for us. Taking our prayer and putting it before her son our Lord Jesus Christ for his divine disposition and asking us to obey it. Not saying we will get what we ask for, or even what she wants, simply leaving it before him. She is in effect prefiguring the words made famous by St Faustina 1900 years later:

Jesus I trust in you!

The final point from the story of the wedding at Cana is more subtle:

3. THE END RESULT OF MARY'S INTERCESSION IS TO BRING PEOPLE TO BELIEF IN HER SON.

On first examination, most people would if asked what the critical result of Mary's intervention on behalf of the couple would be Jesus' direct action on their behalf. But if we focus on the miracle itself, the water becoming wine and the couple being saved from embarrassment (other than the steward thinking they've managed their wine foolishly) we miss the most vital effect of Mary's action.

The significant result of Mary's intervention given ins the very last phrase of the passage, John Chapter 2 verse 11b:

And his disciples began to believe in him.

That is the star of the show, that the wine doesn't run out and embarrass the newlyweds is nice, but you'll note their reaction, were they grateful, were they surprised, were they confused, is not noted in scripture because it's not what counts. What counts, what divine scripture inspired by the Holy Spirit highlights is the ultimate end result of going to Mary as illustrated by sequence of events.

1. **MARY ASKS FOR GOD'S INTERCESSION**

2. **MARY ASKS FOR MAN TO OBEY HER SON**

3. **THE SERVANTS FOLLOW THE LEAD OF JESUS AS MARY TOLD THEM**

4. **JESUS' DISCIPLES BEGIN TO BELIEVE.**

I have heard sermon after sermon where a Catholic priest says that Mary will always lead us to her son, but we don't need a sermon to know this, because we have a direct example in inspired scripture that the intercession of Holy Mary, the Mother of God increases belief in Jesus Christ.

And for Christians that's what it's all about.

So in summation we see:

- Requesting intercessory prayer of one for another, particular a holy one is consistent with scripture

- Mary is an excellent choice for intercessory prayer

- Mary as the humble intercessor who brings people closer to her son is directly demonstrated in scripture

And that end result, causing people to believe in Christ is the primary duty of all Christians.

Part 6
The Timely Intervention

Now, and at the hour of our death, Amen.

Screwtape: I am not in the least interested in knowing how many people in England have been killed by bombs. In what state of mind they died, I can learn from the office at this end. That they were going to die sometime, I knew already.

C S. Lewis The Screwtape Letters #24

Q: It's two days before your unfortunate encounter with a Nausicaan sword. You have that long to make whatever changes you wish. If you can avoid getting stabbed through the heart this time, which I doubt, I will take you back to what you think of as the present. And you can go on with your life with a real heart.

Capt Picard: Then I won't die?

Q: Of course you'll die. It'll just be at a later time.

Star trek TNG Tapestry 1993

The final line of the Hail Mary is in a sense derivative of the previous line. Unlike other parts this line doesn't assert a particular fact (The Lord is with thee), the status of Mary (Holy Mary) or a particular request (Pray for us). It instead notes and requests that the prayers of the Blessed Mother be made at two particular times. We will now examine those two moments where this prayer is asked for.

A. NOW

The importance of <u>now</u> is discussed in the **Old Testament by the Lord himself**:

> If the wicked man turns away from all the sins he committed, if he keeps all my statutes and does what is right and just, he shall surely live, he shall not die. None of the crimes he committed shall be remembered against him; he shall live because of the virtue he has practiced.
>
> Do I indeed derive any pleasure from the death of the wicked? Says the Lord God. Do I not rather rejoice when he turns from his evil way that he may live?
>
> And if the virtuous man turns from the path of virtue to do evil, the same kind of abominable things that the wicked man does, can he do this and still live? None of his virtuous deeds shall be remembered, because he has broken faith and committed sin; because of this, he shall die.

> You say, "The Lord's way is not fair!" Hear now, house of Israel: is it my way that is unfair, or rather, are not your ways unfair? When a virtuous man turns away from virtue to commit iniquity, and dies, it is because of the iniquity he committed that he must die.
>
> But if a wicked man, turning from the wickedness he has committed, does what is right and just, he shall preserve his life; since he has turned away from all the sins which he committed, he shall surely live, he shall not die.
>
> *Ezekiel 18:21-28*

Note that the standard that is being used, for judging good or ill by the Lord is the standard of <u>now.</u>

Paul also uses that very same standard in his **1st letter to the Corinthians:**

> Do you not know that the unjust will not inherit the kingdom of god? Do not be deceived; neither fornicators nor idolaters nor adulterers nor boy prostitutes nor practicing homosexuals nor thieves nor the greedy nor drunkards nor slanderers nor robbers will inherit the kingdom of God. That is what some of you used to be; but now you have had yourselves washed, you were sanctified, you were justified in the name of the lord Jesus Christ and in the spirit of our God.
>
> *1 Corinthians 6:9-11*

Note the Paul lists a multiple of mortal sins. Sins that will get a man burned for all eternity.[5] He also notes that these sins have been committed by the very same Corinthians that he is writing to. Yet as far as he is concerned, they are all in the past, washed away by the blood of Christ. No matter what the past might be the <u>now</u> is what matters.

In this Paul is echoing Christ in the sermon on the mount on the importance of now:

> Can any of you by worrying add a single moment to your life-span? Why are you anxious about clothes? Learn from the way the wild flowers grow. They do not work or spin. But i tell you that not even Solomon in all his splendor was clothed like one of them. If god so clothes the grass of the field, which grows today and is thrown into the oven tomorrow, will he not much more provide for you, o you of little faith?
>
> So do not worry and say, 'what are we to eat?' or 'what are we to drink?' or 'what are we to wear?' all these things the pagans seek. Your heavenly father knows that you need them all. But seek first the kingdom (of God) and his righteousness, and all these things will be given you besides. Do not worry about tomorrow; tomorrow will take care of itself. Sufficient for a day is its own evil.

---

5 The difference between Mortal and Venial Sin has been with the Church from the beginning as Illustrated in the first letter of John, the Mortal sin that leads to death the Venial Sin that does not. Both are to be avoided but only the Mortal sin concerning grave matter, done deliberately and with full understanding breaks the bond of salvation to such a degree that explicit repentance is necessary to reestablish it.

Matthew 6:27-34

The past is already over, the future hasn't happened; the only time that matters is the now. The present is the moment when both sin and virtue takes place. It's the place where the enemy deploys his temptation, many of them designed to get our minds away from the now to either dwell in the past or worry about the future when it is this moment, the now, when we need the intercession because the <u>now</u> is the only time that we can act for good or ill.

Could there be better time to ask for the intercession of the Mother of God?

As a matter of fact there is another time when the intercession of the Mother of God might be more important, and that time is the second specified in the final line of the Hail Mary

B. THE HOUR OF OUR DEATH.

Lord Jesus Christ! Thou Son of God and son of the Virgin Mary, God and man! Thou who in fear sweated blood for us on the mount of olives in order to bring peace and to offer thy most holy death to God, thy heavenly Father, for the salvation of this dying person…if it be however that by his sins he merits eternal damnation, then may it be deflected from him. This, o eternal father, though our lord Jesus Christ, thy dear son, who liveth and reigneth in the union with thee and the holy spirit, now and forever. Amen.

Prayer for the dying Pieta Prayer book

While it might seem odd to say so the hour of our death is in fact the most important moment of our lives. It is the final opportunity for any soul to make peace with God and obtain his mercy. It is the moment when we make the final choice between God's mercy and his justice.

Christ talked of the hour of death and storing up treasure for it in this parable

> Then he said to the crowd, "Take care to guard against all greed, for though one may be rich, one's life does not consist of possessions."
>
> Then he told them a parable. "There was a rich man whose land produced a bountiful harvest. He asked himself, 'what shall I do, for I do not have space to store my harvest?'

And he said, 'This is what I shall do: I shall tear down my barns and build larger ones. There I shall store all my grain and other goods and I shall say to myself, "Now as for you, you have so many good things stored up for many years, rest, eat, drink, be merry!"

But god said to him, 'You fool, this night your life will be demanded of you; and the things you have prepared, to whom will they belong?' Thus will it be for the one who stores up treasure for himself but is not rich in what matters to God."

Luke 12:15-21

Likewise, St Paul was very conscious of this and wrote of it in his first letter to **the Corinthians**:

Do you not know that the runners in the stadium all run in the race, but only one wins the prize? Run so as to win. Every athlete exercises discipline in every way. They do it to win a perishable crown, but we an imperishable one. Thus, I do not run aimlessly; I do not fight as if i were shadowboxing. No, I drive my body and train it, for fear that, after having preached to others, I myself should be disqualified.

1 Cor 9:24-27

and wrote to Timothy of finishing the race as he prepared to die

For I am already being poured out like a libation, and the time of my departure is at hand.

> I have competed well; I have finished the race; I have kept the faith. From now on the crown of righteousness awaits me, which the lord, the just judge, will award to me on that day, and not only to me, but to all who have longed for his appearance.
>
> *2 Timothy 4:6-8*

But beyond all other times it is on the cross itself that Christ demonstrates the effectiveness of prayer at the hour of death:

> Now one of the criminals hanging there reviled Jesus, saying, "are you not the messiah? Save yourself and us."
>
> The other, however, rebuking him, said in reply, "Have you no fear of god, for you are subject to the same condemnation? And indeed, we have been condemned justly, for the sentence we received corresponds to our crimes, but this man has done nothing criminal."
>
> Then he said, "Jesus, remember me when you come into your kingdom." He replied to him, "Amen, I say to you, today you will be with me in paradise."
>
> *Luke 23:39-43*

Christ answer this prayer, the final petition of any made to him. It was by this prayer, this plea for mercy and that statement of faith, made ironically at the hour of both of their deaths, that makes St. Dismus who he is today and confirms the words of Sirach

> Call no man happy before his death, for by how he ends, a man is known.

Sirach 11:28

The Hour of our death is our last chance to accept the outreached hand of God, it is the final gasp that we get our ultimate shot to repent.

And that's what those closing words in the Hail Mary do. Those words follow Christ's advice to store up treasure in heaven, treasure that will not tarnish, treasure that at the hour of death, can be called upon to obtain that requested intercession at the final time that it can be effective.

Unlike St Dismus most of us will not know the hour of our death. It is very possible, even that we will not be in a position to even ask for the mercy of God when that hour comes.

In asking for Mary to pray for us now, we ask Mary to pray with us, in asking for Mary to pray for us at the hour of our death we are asking her to pray for us.

At both times it is a most timely intervention, an intervention that every Christian should be happy to have, particular when we do not know the day or the hour when our time will come.

Part Seven
The Surest Path

From Mary we learn to surrender to God's Will in all things. From Mary we learn to trust even when all hope seems gone. From Mary we learn to love Christ her Son and the Son of God!

Saint John Paul II

And so we have finished our examination of that most Catholic of prayers the Hail Mary, and while I hope you have gotten some new insights on the Hail Mary, the real story is the insights on Mary herself.

To examine the Hail Mary is to examine Mary and to examine Mary is to examine the path of the true Christian.

We understand that Mary is in fact the first Christian, the first called and the first answer yes.

We understand that Mary is above the angels who defer to her in ways that they do not to others.

We understand that Mary is recognized by others who have been called by God.

And yet what do we see? We see Mary rather than Lording over others, praising God in humility, approaching her son humility, deferring to him and most importantly leading Jesus' disciples to belief. This is no surprise for who would have been the biggest human influence on Jesus in his lifetime? Who raised him, was there for him as he learned to walk, learned to talk, and comforted him when he fell? Who taught him to pray, and showed by example the love of the father to complement his divine nature until the time of his mission came?

Mary, will always lead you to Christ because she was not only the first to follow this road but she was the woman who God himself choose to help prepare him for the path that he would walk for the sake of our salvation.

That is the real secret of Mary and Marian devotion a secret hidden in plain sight, A devotion that begins with a single Hail Mary.

And that's why the Devil does his best to keep it hidden.

Appendix:
The Rosary

"Lord, teach us to pray just as John taught his disciples."

Luke 11:1b

The Rosary consists of the following Prayers in the following Sequence

Opening Prayers

The Apostle's Creed:

> I believe in God, the Father Almighty, Creator of heaven and earth. I believe in Jesus Christ, His only Son, our Lord: He was conceived by the power of the Holy Spirit, and born of the Virgin Mary. He; suffered under Pontius Pilate, was crucified, died and was buried. He descended into hell; On the third day He rose again. He ascended into heaven, is seated at the right hand of the Father He will come to judge the living and the dead. I believe in the Holy Spirit, the Holy Catholic Church, the communion of Saints, the forgiveness of sins, the resurrection of the body, and life everlasting. Amen.

The Our Father:

> Our father, who art in heaven, hallowed by thy name. Thy kingdom come, thy will be done on earth as it is in heaven. Give us this day our daily bread and forgive us our trespasses as we forgive those who trespass against us. And lead us not into temptation, but deliver us from evil.

The Hail Mary x 3

> Hail Mary, full of grace, the Lord is with thee. Blessed art thou among women and blessed is the fruit of they womb Jesus. Holy Mary mother of God pray for us sinners, now and at the hour of our death, Amen.

The Glory Be

> Glory Be to the Father, and the Son, and the Holy Spirit, as it was in the beginning is now and ever shall be, world without end Amen.

A decade of the Rosary consists of the following prayers

- The declaration of the Mystery
- Optional opening prayer (variable)

- The Our Father

- The Hail Mary x 10

- The Glory Be

- The Fatima Prayer (Optional) Oh my Jesus, forgive us our sins, save us from the fires of hell and lead all souls into heaven especially those in most need of thy mercy.

- Optional variable Closing prayer

While one can pray an individual decade at any time Rosaries are commonly prayed in groups of five decades consisting of a Mystery. When prayed in this fashion after the 5th decade of a Mystery you close with the Hail Holy Queen

Hail Holy Queen Mother of Mercy, our live our sweetness and our hope, to thee do we cry, to they do we send up our sighs moaning and weeping in this vale of tears. Turn then thy most gracious advocate thine eyes of mercy toward us and show us to the blessed fruit of your womb Jesus. Oh clement, Oh loving oh sweet Virgin Mary. Pray for us holy mother of God that we may be made worthy of the promises of Christ.

Most people who pray the Rosary pray a set of Mysteries. These various Mysteries are traditionally assigned (but not required) to be prayed on a specific day.

Joyful Mysteries: (Traditionally prayed Mondays, Saturdays, Sundays of Advent, and Sundays from Epiphany until Lent)

1. The Annunciation: Gabriel visits Mary

2. The Visitation: Mary Visits Elizabeth

3. The Birth of Jesus

4. The Presentation in the Temple (Jesus is presented in the Temple)

5. The Finding of the Child Jesus in the Temple

Luminous Mysteries: (Traditionally Prayed Thursdays all year)

1. The Baptism of Christ

2. The wedding at Cana

3. The Proclamation of the Kingdom of Heaven

4. The Transfiguration

5. The Institution of the Holy Eucharist at the Last Supper

Sorrowful Mysteries: (Traditionally prayed Tuesdays, Fridays, and daily from Ash Wednesday until Easter Sunday)

1. The Agony in the Garden

2. The Scourging at the Pillar

3. The Crowning with Thorns

4. The Carrying of the Cross

5. The Crucifixion

The Glorious Mysteries (Traditionally Prayed Wednesdays, and Sundays throughout the year)

1. The Resurrection

2. The Ascension of Our Lord

3. The Descent of the Holy Spirit

4. The Assumption of Our Lady into Heaven

5. The Coronation of the Blessed Virgin Mary

It is not uncommon to pray a full 20 decade Rosary with the Hail Holy Queen at the end of each set of Mysteries. (I can do one in about 30 minutes).

At the end of a rosary this optional prayer is commonly prayed by just about everybody.

> O God, whose only-begotten Son, by His Life, Death, and Resurrection has purchased for us the rewards of eternal life; grant, we beseech You, that, meditating on these mysteries of the most holy Rosary of the Blessed Virgin Mary, we may imitate what they contain, and obtain what they promise. Through the same Christ our Lord. Amen.

By just about everybody I mean pretty much everyone I know except for me. I instead pray the opening prayers in reverse order and dedicate them to the prayer intention of the Pope (and since the resignation of Benedict XVI the Pope Emeritus)

- Glory Be

- Hail Mary x 3

- Our Father

- Apostles Creed

But there is no reason why you can't do my method and *then* close with the traditional prayer. Frankly the only reason why I never did so myself is because for the life of me I've never been able to remember that traditional closing prayer off the top of my head so I started using my alternate method and decided to stick with it. It's particularly handy when one is trying to obtain an indulgence[6] since they require prayers for the current intentions of the sitting Pope.

---

6   An indulgence is the remission of the temporal punishment of sins already forgiven, a person acquiring such an indulgence can apply it to either themselves or a person who is deceased currently in purgatory to speed their final passage from purgatory to heaven. The catholic doctrine of purgatory, the need to purge oneself of sin before entering heaven is well established both in tradition and in scripture (Isaiah 6 5-7), (2 Maccabees 12:39-45) and implied in Christ parable mentioned in both Matthew (5:25-26) and Luke (12-58-59) ending in I say to you, you will not be released until you have paid the last penny." The concept is one of the most misunderstood by non-Catholics It's best thought of as a storeowner choosing not to prosecute a vandal but having said vandal pay for what they broke but a proper discussion of the doctrine is deserving of its own volume.

You can also do a "do it yourself" Rosary consisting of whatever decades you wish. In addition to my standard rosary I do a set of "do it yourself" decades daily for a group of specific personal intentions that correspond to the decades I pray.

Remember how you pray the rosary, whether a single decade or a full 20 decades in a day is less important than THAT you pray the rosary. As Paul said to the Thessalonians:

> Pray without ceasing.
>
> *1 Thessalonians 5:17*

I can't think of better words of advice to close with.

Made in the USA
Lexington, KY
11 December 2017